UTTERLY LUCID

JAPNIT KAUR

ISBN 979-888591728-5

This book is dedicated to my Mumma- Gurnish Kaur and Papa-
Gagandeep Singh for being my constant support in life and my
supportive readers for accompanying me on this journey!

Yes, it is dedicated to you!

Contents

Contents

Contents

Contents

Preface

First of all thank you so much for taking some time out of your busy schedule to read my work. So let's know about each other. I'll start first!

I, Japnit Kaur am a 16 year old highschool student. Writing for me is therapy. The first poem that I had written got published in one of the largest national daily The Hindustan Times in the school times section.

I published my first poetry book- 'Bloom- a process of becoming yourself' back in November 2019. I have seen a beautiful growth in my writing style since.

I have also started with an online literary magazine 'Nestled' where I publish the alluring pieces written by writers from all around the globe. I have started it to promote writers, as many writers out there who write beautifully but they don't have an audience. So I wanted to provide them with a platform where they can publish their work for free and they get an audience who wants to read their deserving work.

I have also participated in the Prime Minister's YUVA Scheme. My writing journey started when I was trying to search a poem for the class assembly but could not find one so I tried writing it on my own with little help as it was my first time com posing a poem and I never knew that day would change my life totally. And that was my first poem, ever since I have been writing my heart out on paper.

I come up with my second book- Utterly Lucid, I would like to take a moment to all the readers and my supporters. This would not have been possible if it weren't for you. The thing is I just used to write my poems anytime of the day I felt that "this has to be written" and before I knew I had a considerable amount of poems to present to you in the form of this book- Utterly Lucid (and I am thankful that you are reading this).

For Publishing Queries

Contact: japnitk99@gmail.com

9212206677

A Note Before You Dig In!

Each and every poem is based on unending experiences that life offers, therefore just like those experiences, none of the poems are perfect.

Yet that you are reading this now I hope you enjoy this journey!

1. It's Depth

The depth of a never ending ocean,
The tattling of water somewhere peaceful,
The talkative silence of the pitter-patter of the raindrops,
The hurt of the unsaid,
The sun drowning into the horizon,
A ship in the middle of an unknown sea,
As huge as a mountain,
As thick as the silence in the cold,
That's how deep poetry is,
And how deeply it touches the shore of my heart...

2. Oxymoron's

• 2 •

The days are easy and difficult
At the same time,
It's new and homely
At the same time,
It feels complete and incomplete
At the same time,
It feels lost and found
At the same time,
It feels good and bad
At the same time,
I'm not sure if I can describe all the oxymoron's I've been feeling.

3. ;

The gigantic white sphere
Perfectly makes us feel its presence
In the dark,
It's white radiant smile
Wants me to look at it
and it's buddies- the stars who don't mimic him for not having
light of his own,
But actually sharing a light in them with the mighty moon,
And make them as full
As they are perfectly accompanied by its stars

4. The Bonne Bouche Of Poetry

The crispy pieces of poetry crumble,
The raspberry cake of pleasure,
with bright pink beetroot sorbet of emotions
which is ready to accompany all the way long,
And that meringue thoughts
which are ready to add up to the other elements to the dish of
poem,
In chocolate pop up sphere of overthinking
which is melted by chocolate ganache of confidence.

5. To prove

Well,
I don't want to live in a world
where I have to prove that,
the thing I do is worth it.

6. A place away

A place away from the nasty lies,
A place away from the selfish world,
A place away from where the widow cries,
A place away from the pain,
A place away from have and have nots,
A place away from human existence,
A place where all I hear is nature taking to me,
A place where nature nourishes me,
A place where I shall wander and write,
A place like my heart's bay shore,
A place where water tattles,
A place where clouds cry tears of happiness
Instead of tears of pain,
Somewhere all I can hear is peace,
Somewhere that doesn't works on money,
Somewhere that proves humans are a creation of nature
And can never overcome their place,
I would like to make a small tree house there and call it my home
in the sheath of nature.
Just in front the water waves kiss my feet
Where the weather acts like a lullaby for me
As I sleep on the mulberry sand covered with leaves,
Aplace where silence is melodious...

A place where I inhale golden air
I wish to go here where the language is of clouds,
Where the vivacious moon smiles at me with the sparkly stars
A place sweeter than sugar,
A place cosier as a blanket,
The most beautiful of the places
I shall go and cherish the real life there…

7. Words

• 8 •

There's like a heap of emotions,
and a never ending pile of thoughts
that I can't put in words.

8. ;

Be
hot pink,
to
my melancholy
darkness.

9. It's about

It's about the tremendously bad things,
It's about the vivaciously good things,
It's about exorbitantly bad times,
It's about ridiculously good times,
The only thing constant is the people who stay in the good n the
bad.

10. Cheers

Cheers to the end,
Cheers to the beginning,
Both are incomplete
without each other.

11. To feel...

To feel every glimpse of the second,
To feel what you'll feel that every day,
It's surreal
Yet so real,
To not know what boundaries that day will touch,
What things miight left untouched,
To start this journey
I have to be alone
But it is my choice,
And i know it is going to be wild,
But i will try to be fearfully dauntleess,
Excited and scared,
That's future
For what's coming...

12. Blank, I feel Blank...

• 13 •

Blank I feel Blank,
I don't know if I'm doing enough,
I don't know if I'm doing good,
I don't know if I'm doing fine,
Guess that's life,
What I know is that I'm doing something,
I really believe that better things are coming my way soon,
But I really do get tired after doing everything and not being able
to get the expected result.
That's what we call fruit of our hard work
Yes I do Question if my actually working hard...

13. ;

Ever seen
the crystals dropping down
Your face ?
Some happy and some sad,
Yes that's what they call tears...

14. The Promise

I don't
promise myself
I won't shatter,
But I do
promise that I will get up and
collect my shattered remains,
I will try to overcome
The consequences of the storm
Even if I'm broken
I won't give up on myself.

15. The world my dear

The world my dear,
Isn't just a bed of roses
But full of a billion tosses,
It's a factory of making you better than the other,
It's what Augustus Waters said "The world isn't a wish granting
factory" my dear
So for this you'll have to sway away your fear
The world counts your failures
And how many times you have succeed
It counts your fears
Not your tears.
The world my dear
Is gonna talk about you unmercifully if you fail,
It's gonna judge the way you are when u succeed
Not just like any other fairy tale,
It's the only ship we all have to sail
The world my dear
Is gonna judge your Hermes,
But it's never gonna see what took you to carry that
The world's not gonna see the hardwork n the commitment in it,
It's gonna judge you if you get down a small car,
It's never gonna see the experienced scar
It's the world dear,

Here the wants are like confetti in the air,
Here the judgy eyes follow you everywhere,
The worldly pleasures you see,
It's world dear
It's the world...
They are gonna praise you when you die,
The haters praise you too
But that doesn't do any good
As it never happened when the soul was in here
It's the world my dear...
They are gonna watch you drown
And not come for help,
They are gonna tell your tears you are weak
They are gonna smash n break you in a million pieces
And when you heal
They're gonna be sorry about it
It's the world my dear
It's the world...

16. A Cup Of Coffee With The Universe

The universe
A thousand galaxies,
A million stars,
A billion emotions,
A trillion thoughts,
The black calm sky,
The moon,
Perfectly skimmed coffee
And me...
:-cup of coffee with the universe-:

17. The Edge

Being on the edge
Is almost not falling,
That is what you have to be thankful for
There's a reason to be thankful in everything
It just takes the right amount of acceptance to peep into it.

18. Today...

Today,
I sit with the universe for a cup coffee
We sit n admire each other's
immeasurable depth.

19. ;

I believe there's some kindness left
In the world,
I still believe
After the Monsters I've seen,
I still believe that everyone has a light of being good in them
It's just that their darkness is overruling.

20. The Masterpiece Ballet

I'm drawing a painting of peaceful and the mesmerising sight
As I see a sugar coated person coming near me and backstabbing
me with a knife
I cry,
I cry n cry,
But it hurts and bleeds all again,
I meet an acquaintance who mentors me while we sit in a lane,
I see so many knifes she's been hurt with
But now it doesn't bleed as much,
Yet her smile is the most beautiful thing I've seen in a while,
She teaches me about life
And the new hurting style,
She tells me about the sins,
And the things people can do easily to hurt the warm hearts.
This gives me cold shivers,
She teaches me that it's okay to cry rivers
She tells me to cry myself out
Healing is a slow process yet satisfactory
She speaks to me in the most kind words ever,
Her words are honey
But not sugar coated,
And that's where I know the difference.
She waives me off saying 'I'll let life teach u the rest'

She blesses n passes by,
Like any other passer by.
I sit there n realise it doesn't hurts as much as it did earlier,
I still cry my heart out,
Well that's my birth right.
It takes time,
but I heal,
I stand,
I grow,
I learn,
I heal,
I walk and carry on
Years pass by
With many knifes I reach the spot I sat when I got hurt for the
first time.
See another one crying over their first,
I mentor him,
And waive by saying 'I'll leave the rest for life to teach'
And bless and pass by
Like any other passer by...

21. Cherish it!

It takes a thousand nerves,
A thousand muscles,
And well -adjusted organs,
And a tons of blood
To make a human alive.
How can someone not cherish this for a lifetime.

22. Horizon

The horizon is deep
and that,
kind of makes it beautiful.

23. Enough

• 26 •

There's so much more in ourselves than we can imagine
Yet we tend to feel we are not enough...

24. Belief

I'll sit
there,
right
there
on the
bench gazing
the stars
and
still believing
in
myself
even when
No one
Will.

25. ;

• 28 •

Oh my darling,
You hate me but I love you
What a duo?!
My haters made me strong
Yes, you made me strong
Thank you for hating me when I wasn't wrong
Thank you for hating me for this long
You are my hater n here I am your lover
Look what have I discovered
Oh still darling you know I've recovered?!
Yes I've got myself rediscovered

26. The Inevitable

• 29 •

Today they celebrate their triumph,
I cherish my loss with integrity.
They might celebrate my loss today,
But tomorrow my rise is inevitable...

27. That Gaze...

• 30 •

Ever caught stars staring back at you,
While you gaze their exquisite existence?!

28. Healing

Healing they say is a persistent process.
A cliche which is true indeed,
It's like bringing back life to the dead roses
Finding yourself in you,
Like adding music to the words,
Adding life to an instrument called heart,
It's giving time to your body to make existence worth it.

29. Pity

I pity the cold hearts
I wonder how cold their nature
Makes them feel with the warm hearts...

30. ;

• 33 •

We're all pieces of poetry
Just trying to find our way back...

31. Forever

Our forever isn't as long as an infinity,
It's just the span of our life,
Make sure you love it !

32. Poetry and Me

• 35 •

As pleasant as a garden full of daffodils,
As the chirping of the birds in the morning,
As the wind around the shore,
As the water that touches your feet,
Is as pleasant as poetry is to me...

33. Do We ?

• 36 •

Do we actually live,
Or are we busy burdens our lungs to survive ?

34. Exquisite Breath

• 37 •

Under a million stars,
A sky full of nostalgia and melancholy darkness,
How exquisite is it to feel your breath and feel the strength of your
own,
It's when the aroma of hot coffee goes slipping into your nostrils
And gives you a tint of liveliness.

35. Irony

• 38 •

There's irony in nature
We try to keep ourselves warm in cold
And cold in warmth

36. Darkness

Darkness has its own language
Ever tried to overview its strength over fear

37. ;

In this world full of fake triumphs
Honest losses are least rewarded

38. Lawful Conspiracy

• 41 •

I sit with the sun and the moon,
To admire their lawful conspiracy of day and night...

39. Ballet 2.0

I sit in a bus
With the best posture I can manage to sit in
Legs crossed, hands folded and shoulders straight
Looking the right amount of nervous and confident
I see so many people at a sight
People of all ages and in different walks of life
I want to talk to each one of them and fulfil all my might
I really want to know their opinions on the game called life
I see an aged lady with a blissful smile on her face
Something in me wants to know about all her positive vibes
As the time passes I come to know that she's a cancer fighter
And has hardly 2-3 months more to live
And still gathering all her sorrow aside
how beautiful she smiles
This definitely makes me believe in magical souls
With experienced soles
Just behind this woman sits a young maiden
With a precise fish tail bun
Looking outside the window sorrowfully
I discover that she's grieving for a family member
As soon as I look at this tender aged girl of about eight years
Sitting quietly in a silent rage
On asking her mother about her mood

I discover that there was nothing big she was just upset about not
being able to buy the doll she wished for
As her mom looked tensed and
It looked as if she was in a desperate need to share with someone
that she's helpless as she's lost her job
I think for a moment
About the different phases of life
Where the girl's problem is not getting a doll
Perhaps for her mother's worry for not being able to feed her own
doll
I hear a man arguing over the phone with her wife
About the unwanted tension at her wife
I can hear his facial expressions scream that he is tired
Here I watch a teenager reading his books with the earphones
plugged in his ears
Somewhere that makes me think about the fresh beginnings in his
life
I see a career oriented magazine
I can understand the nervousness
I can feel the 'will I make the right choice' situation
Something tells me to tell him
that he's doing good and to follow his heart
Here an old man arrives and this boy offers him to sit at his place
as the bus was full
This makes me believe in the good in the future generation
This very man can't stop smiling as he's going to meet his family
after months

And that pleasant smile empowers me
As here I am all ready for my first job interview…
So you see
Everyone has some of the other obstacles in their life

40. We Let...

We let the daffodils talk,
We let the clouds draw,
We let the wind walk,
We let the leaves fall,
We let the sky glow,
We let the rain cry,
We let the humans exist,
As most of us don't make it worth living.

41. I know I will

I'll go through the thorns
I'll go through the horns,
I'll go through the pebbles
I'll go through the rebels,
I'll go the through the fire
I'll go through the ice,
I'll go through the liars
I'll go through the nice,
But I'll make up to what I desire,
I'll wait for the day I'll be proud of what I do.

42. ;

• 47 •

I'll
Stand
There
And
Let
Poetry
Sink
In...

43. Warmth

The long nostalgic sleeves
Covering my palms perfectly,
Shoulders moulded,
My favourite comfy ware hugging my body,
Hair rolling down my shoulders,
Trying to sink in the warmness and coldness all at once...
I can feel myself there,
Exactly in that moment,
I want the time to pause or freeze for a moment or two
And just inhale and exhale,
And continue participating in the game
I don't know why this picture,
Just a normal click
Has a connection with me
A deep one,
Every time I feel it,
Yes, that perfectly imperfect picture....
I feel a tint of lavender,
The scent of the candles comes rushing into my nostrils
And again remind me of something,
I still don't get what it is,
But I feel something really deep
It's just that warm cozy night...

44. Ballet 3.0

TI walk down the road with my
Broad shoulders imperfectly upright,
There's so much I see at a sight,
I come across a person who I'd consider my well wisher, he directed me a way
To walk on,
At first piece of thought I think kind of him
As he tried to convey that if I walk in between the road a car might hit and scorn.
He gives me the directions written on crinkly yellow pages with the edges torn
Something told me I could trust the traveller,
As I walk on the directions directed
I discover I'm on top of a mountain hill
With hardly an inch or two to stand by,
That's exactly where life sighs n whispers 'he wasn't trying to help u but he actually wanted u out of the race,
I smirked as I this thought slided through my mind.
I accidentally trought over a rock
And for a moment I thought I heard a death knock,
The other minute I find myself holding this branch protruding from nowhere
And I exactly know god's helping

I shouted for help !
A man with dollars tied with ropes n ropes walking to the other
high of the hill
He glanced at me,
But walked as a passer-by
He was afraid he'd lose a dollar or two by helping me
And the protruding branch cracks a bit
Just like my heart looking at the irony in the word humanity
As I shout for help
So many people pass by
Some of them I'd actually mistaken as my well wishers
They just being the perfect kind of sympathy and showing pity
But not trying to help
Then I meet a person with the perfect beauty
And he had the ropes but was afraid he would spoil his hands in
order to drag me up.
It's then I noticed the branch cracks a bit after every person who
walks ignoring to help me
Maybe god's trying to tell me something in his own designed
way...
Now my branch stands on one end
One more person ignores
And it appears as if my life is over
Then this physically challenged girl
Desires to help me,
She took a bit long
But she didn't give up

And saved my life.

She's the one I didn't know but actually was such a good person by heart and helped me survive!

I exactly get what's god is trying to teach me

Help others but be careful of every Venice flytrap you come across....

45. ;

• 52 •

It feels so good to see yourself healed
It feels so beautiful to see brisk, snappy, peppy me
It feels lovely...
A month ago I was here reading those depressing, in pain, full of war and guilt quotes
Life seemed to me like a wrecking boat
Losing some unwanted people got me so much pain
God directed me right that every effort of mine trying to let those people stay will go in vein
Because somewhere all they caused me was pain
And they didn't deserve to be in my 'main'
My eyes with tears used to rain
N here I am back again the person with a million dollar smile

46. Enough

As free as the sky,
As enough as the sun,
As bright as the moon,
As sparkly as the stars,
As full as the universe...

47. Healed

How I know I've healed?
I smile, the real smile
I wake up every morning not thinking if we will sort out today
but thinking I won't worry about it any day
I've shown all the unwanted fake people the way out.
All they gave me was hatred more and more,
I really don't need people who simply hate
I have started loving my very own self the way I never did
I have stopped apologising
while it's not my fault
I take my stand every time even if it turns out to be revolt,
I have a heart which is not filled with guilts of losing people
Because now for me they don't really exist.

48. I'm Happy!

I'm happy!
I'm happy even if I'm alone,
I'm happy even if I'm the only one with myself,
I'm happy that I survived a mess,
I'm happy that this made me more strong !
I'm happy that I rectified how ruthless people could be
I'm proud of my very own self
I'm glad that I found a different side of me that these haters helped
me find
I'm happy I've healed...

49. ;

• 56 •

It's the moments,
The memories,
The crystal thoughts
All the cherry times
It's about us,
It's about the pain and laughter
You think of the past
And at times you want to replay a moment or two
Or skip some
But everything has taught us something of significant importance
We do realise it someday
cherish your laughter
Cherish your smile
You won't come to know when it will run over a mile

50. Trapped

• 57 •

I don't feel good
I feel trapped in the sea and not being able to escape
But still smiling,
Cause I know that even a few water rattles see me cry then they
will mistake me as weak,
Though the whole Sea knows that she's the definition of strength.
The winds kiss me by my messy hair n whisper in my ear "even if
you are alone you are enough for yourself"
The Sky above smiles n indicates "you will heal, you are healing,
you are better than yesterday, you will be best soon"
And below my ship seeing me has decided not to wreck n gift me
life,
Even the ship's seen me thrive.

51. An Apology

An apology maybe can make things better
But an apology can't undo what's been done,
An apology is a win for the one who's been hurt once
An apology can't demand the same trust again,
An apology is an alliteration just like true trust but everything
just can't be the same
An apology is a token of realisation
But not a fixation of what's already been done,
An apology can lower down the person's frustration
But 'the trust will be the same' is a beautiful misconception,
An apology, realisation, the feeling of being guilty and sorry
If comes naturally then definitely you can be forgiven,
But remember trust is already prisoned n that lock of your
disrespect is was so strong that you yourself can't break it now
Somewhere maybe you will have to live with a guilt
Just as they say trust is not easily built
But breaks it at once into sand and stilt.

52. Broken

"Broken" I said
I feel broken,
Broken n left all alone,
To my actual self I feel so unknown,
All day all I do is mourn...
I have got the guilt of loosing you always in my vains
Every night I let my eyes heavily rain,
I'm tired of making efforts to get you back
I want my life to get back to track
I know you care
It's okay if you don't want to show it
I'll feel it
I was wrong

53. Are They ?

Are some
People
Too good
To
Be true
Or it's just
Not too good
To be like
Some
Of
You
Does this
Sound
Something
New?!

54. ;

The ticking of a clock
The burning of a matchstick
The sound of a heartbeat
depict the importance of moments better than anything...

55. ~Dear Universe~

• 55 •

I shared my heart with you today
As if you were sitting just beside me
As if you were reading what I was hastily writing in that very moment
In the most simplest and shortest way
In a peculiar way only you can understand
You know there were so many other things I could've said in that moment
But instead I said what I said
I know you and me we have an eternal bond
But today I just knew that whatever I was sharing would be true one day
Thank you for today

56. She Smiles

She smiles...
She smiles even on the darkest of nights
She smiles even when for her the sky cries
She smiles when she knows the truth still listening the lies
She smiles when she's seen all her fake allies
She smiles after suffering miles
At times I wonder how she fakes up all these smiles
She hides her true emotions with a smile
A smile...
A smile...
A fake smile....
She smiles while being misjudged
She smiles seeing people have a grudge
She smiles seeing her best friend leave her
She smiles on her unhappy Lady Luck
She smiles when her mind's a mess
Still she smiles...
Still she tries to make things normal with smiles she tries
She smiles while crying at times
Trying to tell the tears not to break her
Deep down, she knows she's seen enough
Deep down, she's discovered she's tough
But somewhere she also feels broken

Somewhere she wants to be isolated
Somewhere she's tired by faking smiles
Somewhere she's tired listening to lies
Somewhere she has a message for all her fake allies
Somewhere behind that strong girl a suffering heart lies...

57. The Lil Things

• 65 •

Little Things that comfort me

. *Poetry*

. *Coffee*

. *Jazz*

. *Mountains*

. *Rain*

.*Scented Candles*

. *Good Food*

58. ;

• 66 •

Why do we talk it fairy tales
Is it our utopian vision?
Why do we imagine happily ever after
Is it an illusion?

59. A Note To The Shattered Ones

I found this piece of someone's trust lying on the floor,
I think it could be yours
So here's a message for you !
I can see the gloomy face not smile,
I can see the swollen eyes,
I could actually hear your cries
Listen up,
"This shall too pass" someone said it right
Believe me you will be happy again
Believe me for some people you don't need to cut your vein
All your loyalty and kindness did not actually go into vain
All they left you with was a stain
Which won't last long
I know you weren't wrong
For being Loyal and caring and not having ego
Maybe they couldn't bare this much kindness for long…

60. That Dream

We all dream
We all imagine that "One day…"
That one day does scare us to death,
But we know it's worth it…
We try hard,
Very hard,
And then one day we pat our selves
For
Making that day breathe...

61. Realisation

Ever felt your breath ?
Ever felt your smile ?
Ever felt that peace inside you ?
Ever felt that you are not in the rat race ?
Ever took a minute to appreciate every second ?
Ever felt what it feels like being alive again ?
Ever felt your heartbeat ?
Well now that's gonna make you realise a ton of things.

62. In The End

In the end of my story
I shall intake my last breath
And cherish it as I would cherish my cheesecake
I shall smile at the sky one last time in flesh,
Before finding my home with them...

63. ;

We all are breathing
Between the
Evitable and the inevitable,
And we are alive
Isn't this treason enough to be grateful for?!

64. Cheers

Cheers to a mountain full of moments,
A heap full of not so good days,
A ocean full of busy days,
A beach full of opportunities,
and a body full of life.

65. She

• 73 •

The sky hugs her in a plethora of colours,
The rainbow admires her not giving up while it rains and shines
altogether,
The sun smiles seeing her shine,
The horizon admires her depth,
The stars glow along with her at dusk,
The moon walks her home and whispers while she falls asleep.
•She really does have a connection with them•

66. Is This Development ?

• 74 •

We think we are doing progress
Undergoing development
Whereas,
all we are doing is running away
from our natural instincts and forms...

67. The Freedom

• 75 •

The freedom to love
The freedom to hate,
The freedom to express
The freedom to cry,
The freedom to laugh
Is all that human existence got...
There's this one freedom that everyone doesn't have,
There's this one freedom that so many people long for,
There's this only freedom that everyone isn't allowed,
There's this paramount freedom,
And this freedom is the freedom of being yourself...

68. ;

This swirlness of breeze that just reached the core of my pennacle
heart,
It got me in the nostalgic mood,
As I would go to the hills- my second home
To cherish this fresh air,
It just feels more refreshing after a long day.

69. The Vow

• 77 •

Under a canopy of warm trees,
A catastrophe of self -love flowers,
Under a sky of generosity,
Beside the flock of kindness,
Near the swarm of pure honey,
Under the blessed sunshine,
In front of the vivid horizon,
I shall take the vow to believe in me every day from dusk to dawn.

70. A Toast

• 78 •

A toast to the ones who belong to themselves,
More than
They belong to anyone else...

71. A Catastrophe

My mind a catastrophe of unending overthinking
Everything I am functions here,
Everything I will be is in here,
Everything I was is in here,
It's just a cliche to say mind is the superpower,
And that it can work in unimaginable ways
But it is Indeed...
It's in here everything that I desire and respire,
It's in here with the things I get pleased
It's all in here I feel....

72. The Story Is Never The Same

Here now the sun is about to wake
As it is dawn,
The moon will dance its goodbye now
But for someone seven seas away,
Things are quite the opposite
-the story is never same for everybody

73. Today

• 81 •

In this world of tomorrows and yesterdays
Let's cherish being in today.

74. 'There'

• 82 •

I'll know I'm there
When I wake up by the breeze hustling their way through the trees
in my garden
By the winds which make the wind chime sing
All the effort to just wake me up to admire their beauty
What a golden pleasure it is to be waken by the nature itself
In the bright shining sun in overwhelming ways
To that place
Where there's sunflowers n cardigans
Such a place that I'm aware of
A place I look upto to call my home

75. ;

• 83 •

Only if we have magic on our fingertips
And faith in our hearts
Blooming flowers in our minds
Our believes in wonderful starts
We can do things which trouble the judgy hollow hearts

76. Tomorrow

Tomorrow,
They say, tomorrow might not be what you imagine it to be
They say, tomorrow might be par what you imagined it to be
But tomorrow they say, is yours to hold
They say, tomorrow might be beautiful
They say, tomorrow might not be like a cherry on top of your cake
But tomorrow they say, is yours to hold
They say, tomorrow might be hard
Tomorrow they say, might be full of turmoils
They say, you might find a way out of the menace maize
But tomorrow they say, is yours to hold
They say tomorrow, you might not be having what you have today
They say tomorrow, you might have what you don't have today
But tomorrow they say is yours to hold
Yet just like they say, tomorrow is mine to hold

77. The Silver Laced Plate

It's surprising how
Little things can make you feel,
There's this something which just flows,
A sensation,
A platinum sensation honeyed with peace
It just makes you feel satisfied
With today,
Perhaps one makes peace
with what tomorrow serves on a silver laced plate.

78. One Of Those Nights

• 86 •

I want one of those nights,
When I just dance it off
On a random street,
Where the guitar plays
I'll laugh a little,
And sway a little,
I'll buy myself roses,
While the melodies still make me fall for them yet again....
And I'll dance a little,
And sway a little,
And cherish my time at the random street,
The street which made me fall in love with living all over again...

79. A wish

Yesterday felt as if there was a wish
In my heart and it got fulfilled,
I felt as full as a moon,
Ignoring all the little pitty imperfections...

80. The Slightest Comfort

Even par a thousand curves,

Even past a billion doubts,

Even past topsy turvy paths of heightened emotions,

In the rainbows and storms,

It's always just me with myself,

But honestly it feels so real and lovely,

Perhaps it's true,

It's true that I am enough, indeed...

I am enough,

As I have the power to make myself feel even the slightest of comfort at the end of the day...

Only if a considerate amount of words existed

To thank you all for reading my creation...